The Sa

The Sayings of
DOCTOR JOHNSON

edited by

BRENDA O'CASEY

DUCKWORTH

First published in 1990 by
Gerald Duckworth & Co. Ltd.
The Old Piano Factory
43 Gloucester Crescent
London NW1

ISBN 0 7156 2352 4

British Library Cataloguing in Publication Data
Johnson, Samuel *1709–1784*
The Sayings of Dr Johnson.
1. English literature. Johnson Samuel, 1709–1784
I. Title II. O'Casey, B.
828.609

ISBN 0-7156-2352-4

Photoset in North Wales by
Derek Doyle & Associates, Mold, Clwyd
Printed in Great Britain by
Redwood Press Limited, Melksham

Contents

We got into a boat to cross over to Blackfriars; and as we moved along the Thames, I talked to him of a little volume, which, altogether unknown to him, was advertised to be published in a few days, under the title of '*Johnsoniana*, or *Bons Mots* of Dr. Johnson'. Johnson: 'Sir, it is a mighty impudent thing.'

Boswell, *Life* 2.432

Introduction

No one is more typical of the eighteenth century – that period of harmony and perfect tension brought to an end, when the elastic broke, by the Romantic Movement – than Samuel Johnson (1709-1784). Johnson was the 'literary Colossus' who straddled the second half of the century, just as Pope had dominated the first. He was 'Dictionary Johnson', Smollett's 'Great Cham of Literature', Foote's 'Grand Panjandrum', Boswell's 'Great Moralist', 'Sage' and 'True-born Englishman': poet, dramatist, essayist, biographer, lexicographer, critic, Latinist, epigrammatist, writer of prologues, prefaces and dedications: above all clubman, 'hardened and shameless tea drinker', master conversationalist.

Johnson's outward appearance was less harmonious than such a profile might suggest. Childhood scrofula had left him scarred and furrowed, partially deaf, blind in one eye, and short-sighted in the other. His huge frame was convulsed by tics. When he walked it was the 'struggling gait of a man in fetters'; on a horse he appeared 'carried as if in a balloon'; often he could be seen gesticulating to no one in particular, or touching posts, or beating with his feet.

Such disabilities, we may imagine, were greater handicaps to genius than anything the Romantics had to contend with: greater, say, than Coleridge's blocked nose, or Byron's club foot. And Johnson also had mental difficulties. Together with his Jacobite and Tory leanings he had inherited from his bookseller father 'a vile melancholy which made him mad all his life, at least not sober'. He suffered a kind of breakdown at the age of 20, and another at 57. His whole life was a losing battle against sloth.

But if the Romantics were willing or eager to let it all hang out, Johnson was in control, if not of his moods and limbs, at any rate of his feelings. His darkest thoughts he confided to his *Prayers and Meditations*; 'mankind he surveyed with extensive view.' Johnson is the supreme representative of the anti-Romantic tendency: the defender of good sense and humanity, the enemy of cant ('a whining pretension to goodness') in all its forms, whether in life or books. Even his religion, to which he clung desperately as an antidote to melancholy and fear of death, was of the rational kind, a superior counterpart of the Great Scheme of Subordination which he believed was essential to health for the body politic.

The appeal of Johnson's character lies in the remarkable union of robust common sense with true tenderness of heart. Johnson hated complainers, as he hated innovators. If patriotism, the cry of frustrated Whigs, was 'the last refuge of a scoundrel', that was because, as Boswell said, it was so often a cloak for self-interest. 'Public affairs vex no man.' And Johnson had seen too much real poverty and suffering to be taken in by 'distresses of sentiment' or 'the cant of sensibility': he abhorred a 'feeler'. However harsh his general principles, he was always kind to individuals, particularly the defenceless and the unfortunate, and always generous with money, if he had any: he loved children ('pretty dears') and beggars: he put pennies in the hands of sleeping urchins.

By nature solitary and a 'rambler', Johnson enjoyed and demanded company; and for company he preferred men of the world to scholars, and ladies of the town to blue-stockings. What he liked best – apart from a well-dressed leg of mutton – was to 'fold his legs and have out his talk'. He would talk readily on any subject that presented itself, from law to divinity to prize-fighting to methods of cookery, brewing or granulating gunpowder. He despised people who 'talked from books', and he judged books by the same standard as he judged people, affectation being the worst crime in both. His view that 'books without the knowledge of life are useless' is admirably exemplified in his own best book, *The Lives of the Poets*, written in old age: his impatience with the 'metaphysical poets', a phrase he coined, his ridicule of the artificialities of 'Lycidas' and Gray's odes, and his balance-sheet of the merits of Dryden and Pope are still among the best things to be found in English criticism.

When Johnson first met his biographer, on Monday 16 May 1763, Boswell was 22, just setting out on the Grand Tour, and Johnson 53. After years of struggle as a bookseller's hack Johnson had established his fame with his moralising essays, *The Rambler* (1750-52), and his great *Dictionary of the English Language* (1755). *The Rambler* was followed by *The Adventurer* (1753-54) and *The Idler* (1758-60), and in 1759 by his only attempt at fiction, *Rasselas*, a pessimistic pseudo-Oriental tale composed 'in the evenings of one week' to defray the cost of his mother's funeral. In July 1962 he had been released from hardship by the grant of a government pension. When he met Boswell he was already in his 'meridian splendour', his only deep sorrow the death eleven years before of his wife Tetty, whom he had married (a widow almost twice his age) in 1735, and whom he mourned to the end.

In the last twenty years of his life, thanks to the pension, Johnson published comparatively little: in 1765 his long-awaited edition of Shakespeare; in 1775 his *Journal to the Western Islands of Scotland*, an account of a tour to the Hebrides made with Boswell (Boswell published his own version in 1785); and in 1779-81 *The Lives of the Poets*, written by accident for the London booksellers.

Johnson devoted himself instead to conversation. With this in mind he founded with his friend Joshua Reynolds the famous 'Club', subsequently the 'Literary Club', whose members included Burke and Goldsmith and later Garrick and Boswell. In 1765 he was taken up by the Thrales. Henry Thrale, a wealthy brewer with 100 acres in Streatham, had recently married the vivacious Hester, a lady of strong literary aspirations. For the next fifteen years, until Thrale died of a well-earned apoplexy (he was a notorious glutton), Johnson was accepted as part of the family and became the centre of an entourage.

After Thrale's death things began to go downhill. In July 1784 Mrs Thrale scandalised her friends by marrying an Italian singer, Gabriel Piozzi. Johnson felt betrayed. His health, already in decline, gradually collapsed, and he died of gout, dropsy and asthma on 10 December.

Fifteen months later Mrs Piozzi published her *Anecdotes*, but Johnson owes his fame almost entirely to Boswell, whose *Life* (1791) is generally regarded as the finest biography in the English language: 'Eclipse is first and the rest nowhere' (Macaulay). Boswell did not attempt to 'melt down his materials into one mass', but employed direct speech to record from his journals the scenes and conversations he had himself lived through, filling in the biographical gaps as best he could from memoranda. Few would deny his claim that in his pages Johnson is seen 'more completely than any man who has ever lived'. This is all the more remarkable when we reflect that, apart from the three months or so in the Hebrides, the two were together on no more than 180 days in twenty years, a fraction of the time Johnson spent with the Thrales.

Johnson regarded conversation as a social contest, and in public, though not in private, would 'talk for victory', resorting where necessary to the most outrageous sophisms to win the day. In the words of a victim: 'He was sometimes jocular, but you felt as if you were playing with a lion's paw ... he had a heavy look; but when he spoke it was like lightning out of a dark cloud.' The brilliance of his talk, as recorded for us by Boswell, is due partly to the unexpected range and direction of his intelligence, and partly to his remarkable readiness to find a parallel or elaborate a metaphor, but also to his very prejudices, which were always displayed with wit – or 'educated insolence' (Aristotle): during a 'tossing and goring' he would often interject a mollifying 'Sir' (or a 'Depend upon it, Sir', when treating a bad case of cant).

Since Johnson's prejudices are so often the right ones, or at any rate acceptable ones (even Boswell endured his remarks about the 'Scotch'), we generally succumb to the sense, while always admiring the force and humour, of what he says. It is difficult to think of anyone who said so much that is worth quoting. That any selection of his 'sayings' derives largely from the *Life* is a tribute to Boswell's genius.

Abbreviations

Adv = The Adventurer; B = Boswell's *Life of Johnson* ed. Hill/Powell (1934) 6 vols (vol. 5 includes Boswell's *Journal of a Tour to the Hebrides*); *D'A = Diaries and Letters of Madame D'Arblay [Fanny Burney], 1778-1840* ed. Dobson (1904) 6 vols; *Idl = The Idler; JM = Johnsonian Miscellanies* ed. Hill (1897) 2 vols (vol. 1 includes *Piozzi's Anecdotes*); *L = Letters of Samuel Johnson, LL.D* ed. Hill (1892) 2 vols; *LP = The Lives of the Poets* ed. Cunningham (1854) 3 vols; *PD = Preface to the Dictionary of the English Language; PS = Preface to Shakespeare; Poems = The Poems of Samuel Johnson*[2] ed. Nichol Smith/McAdam (1974); *Ram = The Rambler; Ras = Rasselas; W = Works* (Oxford 1825) 11 vols; *WI = A Journey to the Western Islands of Scotland* ed. Chapman (1924).

Conversation & Society

There is in this world no real delight (excepting those of sensuality), but exchange of ideas in conversation. *JM* 1.324

That is the happiest conversation where there is no competition, no vanity, but a calm quiet interchange of sentiments. *B* 2.359

[Goldsmith] was not an agreeable companion, for he talked always for fame. A man who does so never can be pleasing. The man who talks to unburthen his mind is the man to delight you. *B* 3.247

Depend upon it, Sir, it is when you come close to a man in conversation, that you discover what his real abilities are. *B* 4.179

Sir, there is nothing by which a man exasperates most people more, than by displaying a superiour ability or brilliancy in conversation. They seem pleased at the time; but their envy makes them curse him at their hearts. *B* 4.195

He ... observed how common it was for people to talk from books; to retail the sentiments of others, and not their own; in short, to converse without any originality of thinking. He was pleased to say, 'You and I do not talk from books.' *B* 5.378

We now have been several hours together; and you have said but one thing for which I envied you. *B* 4.112

Sir, the conversation overflowed and drowned him. *B* 2.122

He used frequently to observe, that men might be very eminent in a profession, without our perceiving any particular power of mind in them in conversation. *B* 4.19

The misfortune of Goldsmith in conversation is this: he goes on without knowing how he is to get off. His genius is great, but his knowledge is small. As they say of a generous man, it is a pity he is not rich, we may say of Goldsmith, it is a pity he is not knowing. He would not keep his knowledge to himself. *B* 2.196

Why, Sir, his conversation does not show the minute hand, but he strikes the hour very correctly [Thrale]. *JM* 2.169

No, Sir; we had *talk* enough, but no *conversation*; there was nothing *discussed*. *B* 4.186

Boswell: But, Sir, may there not be very good conversation without a contest for superiority? Johnson: No animated conversation, Sir, for it cannot be but one or other will come off superiour. *B* 2.444

It is always observable that silence propagates itself, and that the longer talk has been suspended, the more difficult it is to find anything to say. *Adv* no. 84

There is nothing more likely to betray a man into absurdity than *condescension*; when he seems to suppose his understanding too powerful for his company. *B* 4.3

John Wesley's conversation is good, but he is never at leisure. He is always obliged to go at a certain hour. This is very disagreeable to a man who loves to fold his legs and have out his talk, as I do. *B* 3.230

Burke is the only man whose common conversation corresponds with the general fame which he has in the world. Take up whatever topick you please, he is ready to meet you. *B* 4.19

Questioning is not the mode of conversation among gentlemen. *B* 2.472

I will not be baited with *what*, and *why*; what is this? what is that? why is a cow's tail long? why is a fox's tail bushy? *B* 3.268

Depend upon it, Sir, vivacity is much an art, and depends greatly on habit. *B* 2.462

I hate a fellow whom pride, or cowardice, or laziness drives into a corner, and who does nothing when he is there but sit and *growl*; let him come out as I do, and *bark*. *JM* 1.315

When I was a boy, I used always to choose the wrong side of a debate, because most ingenious things, that is to say most new things, could be said upon it. *B* 1.439

The difference, he observed, between a well-bred and an ill-bred man is this: 'One immediately attracts your liking, the other your aversion. You love the one till you find reason to hate him; you hate the other till you find reason to love him.' *B* 4.319

A man should be careful never to tell tales of himself to his own disadvantage. People may be amused and laugh at the time, but they will be remembered, and brought out against him upon some subsequent occasion. *B* 2.472

Nothing is more hopeless than a scheme of merriment. *Idl* 58

Nay, Sir, flattery pleases very generally. In the first place, the flatterer may think what he says to be true: but, in the second place, whether he thinks so or not, he certainly thinks those whom he flatters of consequence enough to be flattered. *B* 2.364

Just praise is only a deft, but flattery is a present. *Ram* no. 155

He that is much flattered soon learns to flatter himself. *LP* 3.188

Never speak of a man in his own presence. It is always indelicate, and may be offensive. *B* 2.472

No man speaks concerning another, even suppose it be in praise, if he thinks he does not hear him, exactly as he would, if he thought he was within hearing. *B* 4.32

Sir, a man has no more right to *say* an uncivil thing, than to *act* one;no more right to say a rude thing to another than to knock him down. *B* 4.28

Mrs. Montagu [the 'Queen of the Blues'] has dropt me. Now, Sir, there are people whom one should like very well to drop, but would not wish to be dropped by. *B* 4.73

One may be so much a man of the world as to be nothing in this world. *B* 3.375

Politeness is fictitious benevolence. It supplies the place of it amongst those who see each other only in publick, or but little. *B* 5.82

Always, Sir, set a high value on spontaneous kindness. He whose inclination prompts him to cultivate your friendship of his own accord, will love you more than one whom you have been at pains to attach to you. *B* 4.115

If a man does not make new acquaintance as he advances through life, he will soon find himself left alone. A man, Sir, should keep his friendship *in constant repair*. *B* 1.300

A friend may often be found and lost, but an *old friend* never can be found, and Nature has provided that he cannot easily be lost. *L* 2.350

Sir, I look upon every day to be lost, in which I do not make a new acquaintance. *B* 4.374

How many friendships have you known formed upon principles of virtue? Most friendships are formed by caprice or by chance, mere confederacies in vice or leagues in folly. *B* 4.280

We must either outlive our friends ... or our friends must outlive us; and I see no man that would hesitate about the choice. *JM* 1.230

The greatest benefit which one friend can confer on another is to guard, and excite, and elevate his virtures. *B* 1.212.

Cling to those who cling to you. *D'A* 7.255

He was a vicious man, but very kind to me. If you call a dog *Hervey*, I shall love him [Henry Hervey, who entertained Johnson during his early obscurity]. *B* 1.106

A very *unclub-able* man [Sir John Hawkins]. *B* 1.480n

Boswell ... is a very *club-able* man. *B* 4.254n

Dear Bathurst ... was a man to my very heart's content: he hated a fool, and he hated a rogue, and he hated a *whig*; he was a very good *hater*. *JM* 1.204

Perhaps the less we quarrel, the more we hate. *B* 3.417

Men hate more steadily than they love. *B* 3.150

I have heard you mentioned as *a man whom everybody likes*. I think life has little more to give [to Boswell]. *B* 3.362

Men & Motives

My dear friend, clear your *mind* of cant ... You may *talk* in this manner; it is a mode of talking in society: but don't *think* foolishly [to Boswell]. *B* 4.221

A man who has been canting all his life, may cant to the last. *B* 3.290

No man takes upon himself small blemishes without supposing that great abilities are attributed to him. *JM* 2.153

A man cannot with propriety speak of himself, except he relates simple facts. *B* 3.323

All censure of a man's self is oblique praise. It is in order to show how much he can spare. It has all the invidiousness of self-praise, and all the reproach of falsehood. *B* 3.323

There lurks, perhaps, in every human heart a desire of distinction, which inclines every man first to hope, and then to believe, that Nature has given him something peculiar to himself. *B* 1.474

Men have a solicitude about fame; and the greater share they have of it, the more afraid they are of losing it. *B* 1.451

Every man has sometime in his life an ambition to be a wag. *D'A* 5.307

Every man has a lurking wish to appear considerable in his native place. *B* 2.141

Depend upon it, Sir, he who does what he is afraid should be known, has something rotten about him. *B* 2.110

No man is angry at another for being inferior to himself. *D'A* 1.65

No man is a hypocrite in his pleasures. *B* 4.316

Men are seldom satisfied with praise introduced or followed by any mention of defect. *LP* 3.81

No, Sir; to act from pure benevolence is not possible for finite beings. Human benevolence is mingled with vanity, interest, or some other motive. *B* 3.48

The fallacy of our self-love extends itself as wide as our interest or affections. Every man believes that mistresses are unfaithful, and patrons capricious; but he excepts his own mistress, and his own patron. *B* 1.381

An infallible characteristic of meanness is cruelty. *B* 4.316

Want of tenderness, he always alledged, was want of parts, and was no less a proof of stupidity than depravity. *B* 2.122

More knowledge may be gained of a man's real character, by a short conversation with one of his servants, than from a formal and studied narrative, begun with his pedigree, and ended with his funeral. *Ram* no. 60

The vanity of being known to be trusted with a secret is generally one of the chief motives to disclose it. *Ram* no. 13

Self-love is often rather arrogant than kind; it does not hide our faults from ourselves, but persuades us that they escape the notice of others, and disposes us to resent censures lest we should confess them to be just. *Ram* no. 155

Histories of the downfall of kingdoms, and revolution of empires, are read with great tranquillity. *Ram* no. 60

Cunning has effect from the credulity of others, rather than from the abilities of those who are cunning. It requires no extraordinary talents to lie and deceive. *B* 5.217

Every man wishes to be wise, and they who cannot be wise are almost always cunning. *Idl* no. 92

Remember that all tricks are either knavish or childish. *B* 3.396

The world has always a right to be regarded. *B* 2.74

The man who threatens the world is always ridiculous; for the world can easily go on without him, and in a short while will cease to miss him. *LP* 3.60

All the complaints which are made of the world are unjust. I never knew a man of merit neglected: it was generally by his own fault that he failed of success. *B* 4.172

Sir, I have never complained of the world; nor do I think that I have reason to complain. It is rather to be wondered at that I have so much. *B* 4.116

With due submission to Providence, a man of genius has been seldom ruined but by himself. *B* 1.381

Never believe extraordinary characters which you hear of people. Depend upon it, Sir, they are exaggerated. You do not see one man shoot a great deal higher than another. *B* 2.450

Depend upon it, Sir, when a man knows he is to be hanged in a fortnight, it concentrates his mind wonderfully. *B* 3.167

Trade could not be managed by those who manage it, if it had much difficulty. *L* 2.126

No, Sir; there is no profession to which a man gives a very great proportion of his time. It is wonderful, when a calculation is made, how little the mind is actually employed in the discharge of any profession. *B* 2.344

We see no qualities in trade that should entitle a man to superiority. We are not angry at a soldier's getting riches, because we see that he possesses qualities which we have not. If a man returns from a battle, having lost one hand, and with the other full of gold, we feel that he deserves the gold; but we cannot think that a fellow, by sitting all day at a desk, is entitled to get above us. *B* 5.328

Foreigners are not a little amazed when they hear of brewers, distillers, and men in similar departments of trade, held forth as persons of considerable consequence. *B* 1.490

A mere literary man is a *dull* man; a man who is solely a man of business is a *selfish* man; but when literature and commerce are united, they make a *respectable* man. *JM* 2.389

Much enquiry having been made concerning a gentleman, who had quitted a company where Johnson was, and no information being obtained; at last Johnson observed that 'he did not care to speak ill of any man behind his back, but he believed the gentleman was an *attorney*.' *B* 2.126

Why, Sir, no man will be a sailor, who has contrivance enough to get himself into a jail; for, being in a ship is being in a jail, with the chance of being drowned. *B* 5.137

When men come to like a sea-life, they are not fit to live on land. *B* 2.438

Every man thinks meanly of himself for not having been a soldier, or not having been at sea. *B* 3.265

Sir, if Lord Mansfield were in a company of General Officers and Admirals who have been in service, he would shrink; he'd wish to creep under the table. *B* 3.265

Reprimand & Invective

Treating your adversary with respect, is giving him an advantage to which he is not entitled ... Sir, treating your adversary with respect, is striking soft in a battle. *B* 5.29

Dearest lady [Hannah More], consider with yourself what your flattery is worth, before you bestow it so freely. *B* 4.341

Sir, you have but two topicks, yourself and me. I am sick of both [to Boswell]. *B* 3.57

Sir, your wife, *under pretence of keeping a bawdy-house*, is a receiver of stolen goods [a humorous example of coarse raillery on the Thames]. *B* 4.26

I would advise you, Sir, to study algebra, if you are not already an adept in it: your head would get less *muddy*. *JM* 1.301

Sir, you see in him vulgar prosperity. *B* 3.410

This lady of yours, Sir, I think, is very fit for a brothel. *B* 3.25

To endeavour to make *her* ridiculous, is like blacking the chimney [of a blue-stocking]. *B* 2.336

She is better employed at her toilet, than using her pen. It is better that she should be reddening her own cheeks, than blackening other people's characters [of a blue-stocking who spent hours putting on rouge]. *B* 3.46

Sir, you talk the language of ignorance. *B* 2.122

Sir, I perceive you are a vile Whig [to Sir Adam Fergusson]. *B* 2.170

Sir, Dr. James did not know enough of Greek to be sensible of his ignorance of the language. *B* 4.33n

Sir, his ignorance is so great, I am afraid to show him the bottom of it. *B* 4.33n

Sir, I have found you an argument, but I am not obliged to find you an understanding. *B* 4.313

Foote is quite impartial, for he tells lies of every body. *B* 2.434

A mind as narrow as a vinegar cruet. *B* 5.269

I'd throw such a rascal into the river [a nobleman's French cook]. *B* 1.469

She was generally slut and drunkard: – occasionally, whore and thief [Bet Flint]. *B* 4.103

The woman's a whore, and there's an end on't [Lady Diana Beauclerk]. *B* 2.247

Like sour, small beer, she could never have been a good thing, and even that bad thing is spoiled. *B* 5.499

That fellow seems to me to possess but one idea, and that is a wrong one. *B* 2.126

Harris ... is a prig, and a bad prig. *B* 3.245

Such an excess of stupidity, Sir, is not in nature [Thomas Sheridan]. *B* 1.453

He fills a chair [a dullard praised by Mrs Thrale]. *B* 4.81

Sir, you know no more of our Church than a Hottentot [to a Presbyterian clergyman]. *B* 5.382

I will not desist from detecting what I think a cheat from any fear of the menaces of a Ruffian [letter to James Macpherson]. *L* 1.307

If he does really think that there is no distinction between virtue and vice, why, Sir, when he leaves our houses let us count our spoons [of Macpherson]. *B* 1.432

I know not indeed whether he has first been a blockhead and that has made him a rogue, or first been a rogue and that has made him a blockhead [Hume]. *B* 5.464

Books & Authors

The chief glory of every people arises from its authors. *PD*

The true genius is a mind of large general powers, accidentally determined to some particular direction. *LP* 1.4

While an author is yet living, we estimate his powers by his worst performance; and when he is dead we estimate them by his best. *PS*

To commence author is to claim praise, and no man can justly aspire to honour, but at the hazard of disgrace. *Ram* no. 93

Every man who writes thinks he can amuse or inform mankind, and they must be the best judges of his pretensions. *JM* 2.7

The wickedness of a loose or profane author is more atrocious than that of the giddy libertine, or drunken ravisher, not only because it extends its effects wider, as a pestilence that taints the air is more destructive than poison infused in a draught, but because it is committed with cool deliberation. *Ram* no. 77

The best part of every author is in general to be found in his book. *JM* 2.310

About things on which the public thinks long it commonly attains to think right. *LP* 2.161

There is nothing more dreadful to an author than neglect, compared with which reproach, hatred, and opposition, are names of happiness. *Ram* no. 2

I would rather be attacked than unnoticed. For the worst thing you can do to an authour is to be silent as to his works. *B* 3.375

It is advantageous to an authour, that his book should be attacked as well as praised. Fame is a shuttlecock. If it be struck only at one end of the room, it will soon fall to the ground. To keep it up, it must be struck at both ends.
B 5.400

I think I have not been attacked enough for it. Attack is the re-action; I never think I have hit hard, unless it rebounds. *B* 2.335

There are few books to which some objection or other may not be made. *B* 3.26

I have ... been often inclined to doubt, whether authors, however querulous, are in reality more miserable than their fellow mortals. *Adv* no. 138

I never did the man an injury; but he would persist in reading his tragedy to me. *B* 4.244n

Boswell: Pray, Sir, have you been much plagued with authours sending you their works to revise? Johnson: No, Sir; I have been thought a sour, surly fellow. Boswell: Very lucky for you, Sir – in that respect. *B* 4.121

A man, who is asked by an authour, what he thinks of his work, is put to the torture, and is not obliged to speak the truth. *B* 3.320

Praise is the tribute which every man is expected to pay for the grant of perusing a manuscript. *JM* 2.192

Never let criticisms operate upon your face or your mind. It is very rarely that an authour is hurt by his criticks. *B* 3.423

Alas, Sir, what a mass of confusion should we have, if every Bishop, and every Judge, every Lawyer, Physician, and Divine, were to write books. *B* 3.182

Authours are like privateers, always fair game for one another. *D'A* 2.212

Sir, there is not a young sapling upon Parnassus more severely blown about by every wind of criticism than that poor fellow [a vain author]. *B* 4.319

An author and his reader are not always of a mind. *LP* 3.231

The promises of authors are like the vows of lovers. *LP* 3.231

There has often been observed a manifest and striking contrariety between the life of an author and his writings. *Ram* no. 14

Men may be convinced, but they cannot be pleased, against their will. *W* 8.26

To a thousand cavils one answer is sufficient: the purpose of a writer is to be read, and the criticism which would destroy the power of pleasing must be blown aside. *LP* 3.129

It is observed that a *corrupt society has many laws*; I know not whether it is not equally true, that *an ignorant age has many books*. *Idl* no. 85

Books without the knowledge of life are useless; for what should books teach but the art of *living*? *JM* 1.324

That book is good in vain that the reader throws away. *LP* 1.375

Boswell: Then, Sir, what is poetry? Johnson: Why Sir, it is much easier to say what it is not. We all *know* what light is; but it is not easy to *tell* what it is. *B* 3.38

Poetry is the art of combining pleasure with truth, by calling imagination to the help of reason. *LP* 1.146

Shakespeare is, above all writers, at least above all modern writers, the poet of nature; the poet that holds up to his readers a faithful mirror of manners and of life. *PS*

He that will understand Shakespeare must not be content to study him in the closet, he must look for his meaning sometimes among the sports of the field, and sometimes among the manufactures of the shop. *PS*

Shakespeare never has six lines together without a fault. Perhaps you may find seven: but this does not refute my general assertion. *B* 2.96

The style of Shakespeare was in itself ungrammatical, perplexed, and obscure. *PS*

It must be at last confessed that, as we owe everything to [Shakespeare], he was something to us; that, if much of the praise is paid by perception and judgement, much is likewise given by custom and veneration. We fix our eyes upon his graces and turn them from his deformities, and endure in him what we should in another despise. *PS*

Corneille is to Shakespeare ... as a clipped hedge is to a forest. *JM* 1.187

About the beginning of the seventeenth century appeared a race of writers that may be termed the *metaphysical poets* ... [they] were men of learning, and to show their learning was their sole endeavour; but, unluckily resolving to show it in rhyme, instead of writing poetry they only wrote verses. *LP* 1.18

In the poem of Hudibras, as in the history of Thucydides, there is more said than done. *LP* 1.180

The want of human interest is always felt. 'Paradise Lost' is one of the books which the reader admires and lays down, and forgets to take up again. None ever wished it longer than it is. *LP* 1.156

Milton, Madam, was a genius that could cut a Colossus from a rock; but could not carve heads upon cherry-stones [to a lady who wondered why the author of *Paradise Lost* should have written such poor sonnets]. *B* 4.305

Surely no man could have fancied that he read 'Lycidas' for pleasure, had he not known its author. *LP* 1.142

Dryden may be properly considered as the father of English criticism. *LP* 1.339

Dryden's page is a natural field rising into inequalities, and diversified by the varied exuberance of abundant vegetation; Pope's is a velvet lawn, shaven by the scythe, and levelled by the roller. *LP* 3.115

Whoever wishes to attain an English style, familiar but not coarse, and elegant but not ostentatious, must give his days and nights to the volumes of Addison. *LP* 2.178

They are too thin ... for an Englishman's taste: mere superficial observations on life and manners, without erudition enough to make them keep, like French wines, which turn sour with standing a while, for want of *body*, as we call it [Steele's Essays]. *JM* 1.187

If Pope be not a poet, where is poetry to be found? *LP* 3.137

Sir, a thousand years may elapse before there shall appear another man with a power of versification equal to that of Pope. *B* 4.46

In this work ['The Rape of the Lock'] are exhibited, in a very high degree, the two most engaging powers of an author. New things are made familiar, and familiar things are made new. *LP* 3.125

If the writer of the 'Iliad' were to class his successors, he would assign a very high place to his translator, without requiring any other evidence of Genius [Pope]. *LP* 3.138

The incessant and unappeasable malignity of Pope. *LP* 3.85

It is praised by the biographers ... I would rather praise it than read it [an early work of Congreve]. *LP* 2.232

Perhaps no writer can easily be found that has borrowed so little, or that in all his excellencies and all his defects has so well maintained his claim to be considered as original [Swift]. *LP* 3.200

The person of Swift has not many recommendations. He had a kind of muddy complexion, which, though he washed with Oriental scrupulosity, did not look clear. *LP* 3.193

Lord Chesterfield's *Letters* to his son, I think, might be made a very pretty book. Take out the immorality, and it should be put into the hands of every young gentleman. *B* 3.53

They teach the morals of a whore, and the manners of a dancing master [ditto]. *B* 1.266

This man I thought had been a Lord among wits; but, I find, he is only a wit among Lords! [Chesterfield]. *B* 1.266

Is not a Patron, my Lord, one who looks with unconcern on a man struggling for life in the water and, when he has reached ground, encumbers him with help? [ditto]. *B* 1.262

Sir, he was a scoundrel, and a coward: a scoundrel, for charging a blunderbuss against religion and morality; a coward, because he had not resolution to fire it off himself, but left half-a-crown to a beggarly Scotchman, to draw the trigger after his death! [Lord Bolingbroke, whose works were published posthumously by David Mallet]. *B* 1.268

Nullum fere scribendi genus non tetigit, nullum quod tetigit non ornavit. 'Scarce any kind of writing did he not attempt: none that he attempted did he not adorn' [from Goldsmith's epitaph]. *B* 3.82

Goldsmith ... was a man, who, whatever he wrote, did it better than any other man could do. *B* 3.253

No man was more foolish when he had not a pen in his hand, or more wise when he had [ditto]. *B* 4.29

His 'Vicar of Wakefield' I myself did not think would have had much success. *B* 3.321

Yes, Sir, many men, many women, and many children [on being asked whether any man of a modern age could have written the poems of Ossian]. *B* 1.396

Sir, a man might write such stuff for ever, if he would *abandon* his mind to it [ditto]. *B* 4.183

They are forced plants, raised in a hot-bed; and they are poor plants; they are but cucumbers after all [Gray's *Odes*]. *B* 4.13

He has a kind of strutting dignity, and is tall by walking on tiptoe. His act and his struggle are too visible, and there is too little appearance of ease and nature [Gray]. *LP* 3.417

In the character of his Elegy I rejoice to concur with the common reader; for by the common sense of readers uncorrupted by literary prejudices, after all the refinements of subtilty and the dogmatism of learning, must be finally decided all claim to poetical honours [ditto]. *LP* 3.417

Sir, he was dull in company, dull in his closet, dull every where. He was dull in a new way, and that made many people think him *great* [ditto]. *B* 2.327

Nothing can be poorer than his mode of writing: it is the mere bouncing of a school-boy [Dalrymple]. *B* 2.210

Sir, there is more knowledge of the heart in one letter of Richardson's, than in all 'Tom Jones'. *B* 2.173

Why, Sir, if you were to read Richardson for the story, your impatience would be so much fretted that you would hang yourself. *B* 2.175

Richardson had little conversation, except about his own works. *B* 4.28

That fellow died merely for want of change among his flatterers: he perished for want of *more,* like a man obliged to breathe the same air till it is exhausted [ditto]. *B* 5.396n

Sir, there is no settling the point of precedency between a louse and a flea [on being asked whether Derrick or Smart was the better poet]. *B* 4.192

Huggins has ball without powder, and Warton powder without ball [of two controversialists one of whom was master of the subject and the other of a good style]. *B* 4.7

Sir, I love Robertson and I won't talk of his book. *B* 2.53

The worst of Warburton is, that he has a rage for saying something, where there is nothing to be said. *B* 1.329

Yes, Sir; if a man were to go by chance at the same time with Burke under a shed, to shun a shower, he would say – 'this is an extraordinary man.' *B* 4.275

Yes; Burke *is* an extraordinary man. His stream of mind is perpetual. *B* 2.450

Sir, I know no man who has passed through life with more observation than Reynolds. *B* 4.6

Young froths, and foams, and bubbles, sometimes very vigorously; but we must not compare the noise made by your tea-kettle here with the roaring of the ocean [of the author of 'Night Thoughts']. *JM* 1.187

Nothing odd will do long. 'Tristram Shandy' did not last. *B* 2.449

Alas, Madam! how few books are there of which one ever can possibly arrive at the *last* page? Was there ever yet anything written by mere man that was wished longer by its readers, excepting Don Quixote, Robinson Crusoe, and the Pilgrim's Progress? [to Mrs Thrale] *JM* 1.332

Burton's 'Anatomy of Melancholy', he said, was the only book that ever took him out of bed two hours sooner than he wished to rise. *B* 2.121

Osborne [a bookseller] was a man entirely destitute of shame, without sense of any disgrace but that of poverty. *LP* 3.89

The booksellers are generous liberal-minded men. *B* 1.304

Reading & Writing

It is strange that there should be so little reading in the world, and so much writing. People in general do not willingly read, if they can have any thing else to amuse them. *B* 4.218

The progress which understanding makes through a book, has more pain than pleasure in it. *B* 4.218

A man ought to read just as inclination leads him; for what he reads as a task will do him little good. *B* 1.428

If a man begins to read in the middle of a book, and feels an inclination to go on, let him not quit it, to go to the beginning. He may, perhaps, not feel again the inclination. *B* 3.43

What is read twice is commonly better remembered than what is transcribed ... The true act of memory is the act of attention. *Idl* no.74

A book may be good for nothing; or there may be only one thing in it worth knowing; are we to read it all through? *B* 4.308

No, Sir; do *you* read books *through*? *B* 2.226

Notes are often necessary, but they are necessary evils. *PS*

We must read what the world reads at the moment ... It must be considered that we have now more knowledge generally diffused; all our ladies read now, which is a great extension. *B* 3.332

No man reads a book of science from pure inclination. The books that we do read with pleasure are light compositions, which contain a quick succession of events. *B* 4.218

Biography is of the various kinds of narrative that which is most eagerly read, and most easily applied to the purposes of life. *Idl* no. 84

I fancy mankind may come, in time, to write all aphoristically, except in narrative; grow weary of preparation, and connection, and illustration, and all those arts by which a big book is made. *B* 5.39

Great abilities are not requisite for an Historian; for in historical composition, all the greatest powers of the human mind are quiescent. *B* 1.424

It has now become so much the fashion to publish letters, that in order to avoid it, I put as little into mine as I can. *B* 4.102

When a man writes from his own mind, he writes very rapidly. The greatest part of a writer's time is spent in reading, in order to write: a man will turn over half a library to make one book. *B* 2.344

Composition is, for the most part, an effort of slow diligence and steady perseverance, to which the mind is dragged by necessity or resolution, and from which the attention is every moment starting to more delightful amusements. *Adv* no. 138

No man loves to be indebted to his contemporaries. *LP* 3.28

No man but a blockhead ever wrote except for money. *B* 3.19

I allow you may have pleasure from writing, after it is over, if you have written well; but you don't go willingly to it again. *B* 4.219

A man should begin to write soon; for, if he waits till his judgement is matured, his inability, through want of practice to express his conceptions, will make the disproportion so great between what he sees and what he can attain, that he will probably be discouraged from writing at all. *B* 4.12

It is a rule never to be forgotten, that whatever strikes strongly, should be described while the first impression remains fresh upon the mind *B* 1.337

A man may write at any time, if he will set himself *doggedly* to it. *B* 5.40

What is written without effort is in general read without pleasure. *JM* 2.309

Grand nonsense is insupportable. *B* 1.402

He that has once studiously formed a style, rarely writes afterwards with complete ease. *LP* 3.64

He that writes much will not easily escape a manner. *LP* 1.346

Composing a Dictionary requires books and a desk; you can make a poem walking in the fields, or lying in bed. *B* 5.47

Nobody can write the life of a man, but those who have eat and drunk and lived in social intercourse with him. *B* 2.166

A new manner! Buckinger had no hands, and he wrote his name with his toes at Charing-cross, for half a crown apiece; that was a new manner of writing! *JM* 1.419

Read over your compositions and whenever you meet with a passage which you think is particularly fine, strike it out [quoting an old college tutor]. *B* 2.237

In lapidary inscriptions a man is not upon oath. *B* 2.407

Tediousness is the most fatal of all faults ... Unhappily this pernicious failure is that which an author is least able to discover. *LP* 2.223

Allegories drawn to great length will always break. *LP* 1.361

Exclamation seldom succeeds in our language; and, I think, it may be observed, that the particle O! used at the beginning of a sentence, always offends. *LP* 3.149

Tom Birch is as brisk as a bee in conversation; but no sooner does he take a pen in his hand, than it becomes a torpedo to him and benumbs all his faculties. *B* 1.159

You *may* abuse a tragedy, though you cannot write one. You may scold a carpenter who has made you a bad table, though you cannot make a table. It is not your trade to make tables. *B* 1.409

It is the great excellence of a writer to put into his book as much as his book will hold ... Robertson is like a man who has packed gold in wool: the wool takes up more room than the gold. *B* 2.237

There are two things which I am confident I can do very well: one is an introduction to any literary work, stating what it is to contain, and how it should be executed in the most perfect manner; the other is a conclusion, shewing from various causes why the execution has not been equal to what the authour promised to himself and to the publick. *B* 1.292

Sir, I never saw the man, and never read the book. The booksellers wanted a Preface to a Dictionary of Trade and Commerce. I knew very well what such a Dictionary should be, and I wrote a Preface accordingly. *B* 1.359

'Sir,' said Johnson, 'I believe that is true. The dogs don't know how to write trifles with dignity' [on being told that he was supreme in biography]. *B* 4.34n

I shall never envy the honours which wit and learning obtain in any other cause, if I can be numbered among the writers who have give ardour to virtue, and confidence to truth. *Ram* 208 [last paragraph of the last 'Rambler']

The English dictionary was written with little assistance of the learned, and without any patronage of the great; not in the soft obscurities of retirement, or under the shelter of academic bowers, but amidst inconvenience and distraction, in sickness and sorrow. *PD*

Boswell: You did not know what you were undertaking [the Dictionary]. Johnson: Yes, Sir, I knew very well what I was undertaking, – and very well how to do it, – and have done it very well. *B* 3.405

Every other author may aspire to praise; the lexicographer can only hope to escape reproach. *PD*

Sir, I have two very cogent reasons for not printing any list of subscribers [to his edition of Shakespeare]; – one, that I have lost all the names, – and the other, that I have spent all the money. *B* 4.111

Some time in March I finished the 'Lives of the Poets', which I wrote in my usual way dilatorily and hastily, unwilling to work, and working with vigour and haste. *B* 4.34

I could write a better book of cookery than has ever yet been written; it should be on philosophical principles. *B* 3.284

Sir, I thought it had been better [on being asked why he had left the room during a reading of his play *Irene*]. *B* 4.5

Too wordy [his own judgment later on a 'Rambler']. *B* 4.5

No, Sir, I am not obliged to do any more. No man is obliged to do as much as he can do. A man is to have part of his life to himself. *B* 2.15

Education & Learning

Why, Sir, I should not much like my company [on being asked what he would do if he were shut up in a castle with a baby]. *B* 2.100

One cannot love *lumps of flesh,* and little infants are nothing more. *JM* 1.328

Babies do not want to hear about babies; they like to be told of giants and castles and of somewhat which can stretch and stimulate their little minds [of Newbery's children's books, such as *Goody Two Shoes*]. *JM* 1.156

Remember always … that the parents buy the books, and that the children never read them. *JM* 1.156

Never ask a baby of seven years old which way *his genius* leads him, when we all know that a boy of seven years old has no *genius* for anything except a peg-top and an apple pye. *JM* 1.314

Children are entertained with stories full of prodigies; their experience not being sufficient to cause them to be so readily startled at deviations from the natural course of life. *B* 4.16

Endeavouring to make children prematurely wise is useless labour. Suppose they have more knowledge at five or six years old than other children, what use can be made of it? *B* 2.407

Sir, it is no matter what you teach them first, any more than what leg you shall put into your breaches first. *B* 1.452

Allow them to be happy their own way: for what better way will they ever find? *L* 2.183

Poor people's children never respect them: I did not respect my own mother, though I loved her: and one day, when in anger she called me a puppy, I asked her if she knew what they called a puppy's mother. *JM* 1.163

I am always for getting a boy forward in his learning; for that is a sure good. I would let him at first read *any* English book which happens to engage his attention; because you have done a great deal when you have brought him to have entertainment from a book. He'll get better books afterwards. *B* 3.385

Madam, to read, to write, to count; grammar, writing, and arithmetic; three things which, if not taught very early in life are seldom or never taught to any purpose, and without the knowledge of which no superstructure of learning or of knowledge can be built. *JM* 2.301

A child should not be discouraged from reading anything that he takes a liking to from a notion that it is above his reach. *B* 4.21

I never frighten young people with difficulties; on the contrary, I tell them that they may very easily get as much as will do very well. I do not indeed tell them that they will be *Bentleys*. *B* 5.316

Accustom your children constantly to this: if a thing happened at one window and they, when relating it, say that it happened at another, do not let it pass, but instantly check them; you do not know where deviation from truth will end. *B* 3.228

The rod produces an effect which terminates in itself. A child is afraid of being whipped, and gets his task, and there's an end on't; whereas, by exciting emulation and comparisons of superiority, you lay the foundation of lasting mischief; you make brothers and sisters hate each other. *B* 1.46

There is now less flogging in our great schools than formerly, but then less is learned there; so that what the boys get at one end they lose at the other. *B* 2.407

Sir, my early years I read very hard. It is a sad reflection, but a true one, that I knew almost as much at eighteen as I do now. *B* 1.445

Johnson: I had no notion that I was wrong or irreverent to my tutor. Boswell: That, Sir, was great fortitude of mind. Johnson: No, Sir: stark insensibility [on excusing his absence from an Oxford tutorial on the grounds that he had been 'sliding in Christ Church meadow']. *B* 1.60

Youth enters the world with very happy prejudices in her own favour. *Ram* no. 127

He maintained that a boy at school was the happiest of human beings. *B* 1.451

Sir, young men have more virtue than old men; they have more generous sentiments in every respect. *B* 1.445

A schoolboy's exercise may be a pretty thing for a schoolboy, but it is no treat for a man. *B* 2.129

Why, Sir, our tastes greatly alter. The lad does not care for the child's rattle, and the old man does not care for the young man's whore. *B* 2.14

Curiosity is, in great and generous minds, the first passion and the last; and perhaps always predominates in proportion to the strength of the contemplative faculties. *Ram* no. 150

Such is the delight of mental superiority, that none on whom nature or study have conferred it, would purchase the gifts of fortune by its loss. *Ram* no. 150

Sir, a desire of knowledge is the natural feeling of mankind; and every human being, whose mind is not debauched, will be willing to give all that he has to get knowledge. *B* 1.458

All knowledge is of itself of some value. There is nothing so minute or inconsiderable, that I would not rather know it than not. *B* 2.357

If it rained knowledge I'd hold out my hand; but I would not give myself the trouble to go in quest of it [excusing himself from a threatened visit by Lord Marchmont who wished to 'communicate all he knew about Pope']. *B* 3.344

Knowledge is of two kinds. We know a subject ourselves, or we know where we can find information upon it. *B* 2.365

A mere antiquarian is a rugged being. *B* 3.278

It will, I believe, be found invariably true, that learning was never decried by any learned man; and what credit can be given to those, who venture to condemn that which they do not know? *Adv* no. 85

He used to quote, with great warmth, the saying of Aristotle recorded by Diogenes Laertius; that there was the same difference between one learned and unlearned, as between the living and the dead. *B* 4.13

All intellectual improvement arises from leisure. *B* 2.19

The true act of memory is the act of attention. *Idl* no. 74

The true, strong and sound mind is the mind that can embrace equally great things and small. *B* 3.334

I have always suspected that the reading is right, which requires many words to prove it wrong; and the emendation wrong, that cannot without so much labour appear to be right. *PS*

Classical quotation is the *parole* of literary men all over the world. *L* 4.102

Greek, Sir, is like lace; every man gets as much of it as he can. *B* 4.23

She had learning enough to have given dignity to a Bishop [Queen Elizabeth]. *B* 4.13

Sir, if a man has a mind to *prance*, he must study at Christ-Church or All-Souls. *B* 2.67

I believe they might be good beings; but they were not fit to be in the University of Oxford. A cow is a very good animal in the field; but we turn her out of a garden [of six Methodist students expelled from Oxford for 'praying and exhorting']. *B* 2.187

Ignorance, Madam, ignorance [to a lady who asked him how he came to define *pastern* in his Dictionary as a horse's *knee*]. *JM* 2.278

What, my dears! then you have been looking for them [to two ladies who expressed their satisfaction that naughty words had been omitted from the Dictionary]. *JM* 2.390

Yet think what ills the scholar's life assail,/ Toil, envy, want, the patron and the jail ['garret' for 'patron' in the first version]. *Poems* 122

Dictionary Definitions

Cant (3): A whining pretension to goodness, in formal and affected terms.

Cough: A convulsion of the lungs, vellicated by some sharp serosity.

Dull (8): Not exhilarating; not delightful: as, *to make dictionaries is dull work.*

Elephant: The largest of all quadrupeds, of whose sagacity, faithfulness, prudence, and even understanding, many surprising relations are given. This animal feeds on hay, herbs and all sorts of pulse; and is said to be extremely long-lived. He is supplied with a trunk, or long hollow cartilage, which hangs between his teeth, and serves him for hands. His teeth are the ivory.

Excise: A hateful tax levied upon commodities, and adjudged not by the common judges of property, but wretches hired by those to whom excise is paid.

Favourite (2): One chosen as a companion by a superior; a mean wretch whose whole business is by any means to please.

Grubstreet: Originally the name of a street, near Moorfields in London, much inhabited by writers of small histories, dictionaries, and temporary poems whence any mean production is called grubstreet.

Lexicographer: A writer of dictionaries; a harmless drudge, that busies himself in tracing the original, and detailing the signification of words.

Network: Any thing reticulated or decussated, at equal distances, with interstices between the intersections.

Oats: A grain, which in England is generally given to horses, but in Scotland supports the people.

Patriot (2): It is sometimes used for a factious disturber of the government.

Patron (1): One who countenances, supports, or protects. Commonly a wretch who supports with influence, and is paid with flattery.

Pension: An allowance made to anyone without an equivalent. In England it is generally understood to mean pay given to a state hireling for treason to his country.

Tory: (A cant term, derived, I suppose from an Irish word signifying a savage.) One who adheres to the ancient constitution of the state and the apostolic hierarchy of the Church of England: opposed to a *Whig*.

Whig (2): The name of a faction.

Women & Marriage

I am much pleased with a compliment, especially from a pretty woman. *B* 4.275

Women have a great advantage that they may take up with little things, without disgracing themselves: a man cannot, except with fiddling. Had I learnt to fiddle, I should have done nothing else. *B* 3.242

If I had no duties, and no reference to futurity, I would spend my life in driving briskly in a post-chaise with a pretty woman; but she should be one who could understand me, and would add something to the conversation. *B* 3.162

I have often thought that if I kept a seraglio, the ladies should all wear linen gowns, or cotton; I mean stuffs made of vegetable substances. I would have no silk; you cannot tell when it is clean. *B* 5.216

I'll come no more behind your scenes, David [Garrick]: for the silk stockings and white bosoms of your actresses excite my amorous propensities ['do make my genitals to quiver', in Wilkes's version]. *B* 1.201

As the faculty of writing has been chiefly a masculine endowment the reproach of making the world miserable has been always thrown upon the women. *Ram* no. 18

Where there is no education, as in savage countries, men will have the upper hand of women. Bodily strength, no doubt, contributes to this; but it would be so, exclusive of that; for it is mind that always governs. When it comes to dry understanding, man has the better. *B* 1.52

When a man says, he had pleasure with a woman, he does not mean conversation, but something of a very different nature. *B* 3.246

Ladies set no value on the moral character of men who pay their addresses to them; the greatest profligate will be as well received as the man of the greatest virtue, and this by a very good woman, by a woman who says her prayers three times a day ... No, no; a lady will take Jonathan Wild as readily as St. Austin, if he has threepence more. *B* 4.291

Women have a perpetual envy of our vices; they are less vicious than we, not from choice, but because we restrict them; they are the slaves of order and fashion; their virtue is of more consequence to us than our own, so far as concerns this world. *B* 4.291

Adventitious accomplishments may be possessed by all ranks; but one may easily distinguish the *born gentlewoman*. *B* 2.130

Nature has given women so much power that the law has very wisely given them little. *L* 1.104

A principle of honour or fear of the world will many times keep a man in decent order; but when a woman loses her religion, she, in general, loses the only tie that will restrain her actions. *JM* 2.309

Gluttony is, I think, less common among women than among men. Women commonly eat more sparingly, and are less curious in the choice of meat; but if once you find a woman gluttonous, expect from her very little virtue. Her mind is enslaved to the lowest and grossest temptation. *L* 2.323

There are ten genteel women for one genteel man, because they are more restrained. A man without some degree of restraint is insufferable; but we are all less restrained than women. Were a woman sitting in company to put out her legs before her as most men do [referring to Boswell], we should be tempted to kick them in. *B* 3.53

Were it not for imagination, Sir, a man would be as happy in the arms of a chambermaid as of a Duchess. *B* 3.341

There are a few things that we so unwillingly give up, even in an advanced age, as the supposition that we have still the power of ingratiating ourselves with the Fair Sex. *JM* 2.326

Clive, Sir, is a good thing to sit by; she always understands what you say [Kitty Clive, 'the best player I ever saw']. *B* 4.7

Sir, Mrs. Montagu does not make a trade of her wit; but Mrs. Montagu is a very extraordinary woman; she has a constant stream of conversation, and it is always impregnated; it has always meaning. *B* 4.275

She does not gain up on me, Sir; I think her empty-headed [a lady at Bath]. *B* 3.48

Poll [Carmichael] was a stupid slut. I had some hopes of her at first, but when I talked to her tightly and closely, I could make nothing of her. She was wiggle-waggle, and I could never persuade her to be categorical. *D'A* 1.114

A man is in general better pleased when he has a good dinner upon his table, than when his wife talks Greek. My old friend, Mrs. Carter, could make a pudding, as well as translate Epictetus. *JM* 2.11

Sir, a woman's preaching is like a dog's walking on his hinder legs. It is not done well; but you are surprized to find it done at all [of a female Quaker]. *B* 1.463

Whoremonger is a dealer in whores, as ironmonger is a dealer in iron. But as you don't call a man an ironmonger for buying and selling a pen-knife; so you don't call a man a whoremonger for getting one wench with child. *B* 2.172

No, Madam. Women can spin very well; but they cannot make a good book of Cookery [to Miss Seward]. *B* 3.286

The woman had a bottom of good sense ... I say the *woman* was *fundamentally* sensible. *B* 4.99

[Milton] thought woman made only for obedience, and man only for rebellion. *LP* 1.135

I do not ... pretend to have discovered that life has any thing more to be desired than a prudent and virtuous marriage. *B* 1.382

A man should marry first, for virtue; secondly, for wit; thirdly, for beauty; and fourthly, for money. *JM* 2.8

An accurate view of the world will confirm, that marriage is not commonly unhappy, otherwise than as life is unhappy; and that most of those who complain of connubial miseries, have as much satisfaction as their nature would have admitted, or their conduct procured, in any other condition. *Ram* no. 45

They that have grown old in a single state are generally found to be morose, fretful, and captious. *Ram* no. 112

Marriage has many pains, but celibacy has no pleasures. *Ras* ch. 26

Notwithstanding all that wit, or malice, or pride, or prudence will be able to suggest, men and women must at last pass their lives together. *Ram* no. 119

Our marriage service is too refined. It is calculated only for the best kind of marriages; whereas we should have a form for matches of convenience, of which there are many. *B* 2.110

The triumph of hope over experience [of a second marriage, after the first had been unhappy]. *B* 2.128

All quarrels ought to be avoided studiously, particularly conjugal ones, as no one can possibly tell where they may end; besides that lasting dislike is often the consequence of occasional disgust, and that the cup of life is surely bitter enough, without squeezing in the bitter rind of resentment. *JM* 1.246

Boswell: Pray, Sir, do you not suppose that there are fifty women in the world, with any of whom a man may be as happy as with any one woman in particular? Johnson: Ay, Sir, fifty thousand. *B* 2.461

Marriages would in general be as happy, and often more so, if they were all made by the Lord Chancellor. *B* 2.461

Marriage, Sir, is much more necessary to a man than to a woman; for he is much less able to supply himself with domestic comforts. *B* 2.471

Confusion of progeny constitutes the essence of the crime [adultery]; and therefore a woman who breaks her marriage vows is much more criminal than a man who does it. A man to be sure, is criminal in the sight of *God*: but he does not do his wife a very material injury, if he does not insult her: if for instance, from mere wantonness of appetite, he steals privately to her chambermaid. Sir, a wife ought not greatly to resent this. *B* 2.55

Sir, a man will not, once in a hundred instances, leave his wife and go to a harlot, if his wife has not been negligent. *B* 2.56

There is, indeed, nothing that so much seduces reason from vigilance, as the thought of passing life with an amiable woman; and if all would happen that a lover fancies, I know not what other terrestrial happiness would deserve pursuit. But love and marriage are different states. *B* 1.381

Sir, it is so far from natural for a man and woman to live in a state of marriage, that we find all the motives which they have for remaining in that connection, and the constraints which civilised society imposes to prevent separation, are hardly sufficient to keep them together. *B* 2.165

Supposing a wife to be of a studious or argumentative turn, it would be very troublesome: for instance, – if a woman should continually dwell upon the subject of the Arian heresy. *B* 4.32

Now that you are going to marry, do not expect more from life, than life will afford. You may often find yourself out of humour, and you may often think your wife not studious enough to please you; and yet you may have reason enough to consider yourself as upon the whole very happily married [to Boswell]. *B* 2.110

No man will be fond of what forces him daily to feel himself inferior [of a sociable man married to a religious wife]. *JM* 1.256

Men know that women are an over-match for them, and therefore they choose the weakest or most ignorant. If they did not think so, they could never be afraid of women knowing as much as themselves. *B* 5.226

Some cunning men choose fools for their wives, thinking to manage them, but they always fail ... Depend upon it, no woman is the worse for sense and knowledge. *B* 5.226

Of the passion of love he remarked, that its violence and ill effects were never exaggerated; for who knows any real sufferings on that head, more than from the exorbitancy of any other passion? *B* 2.122

It is commonly a weak man who marries for love. *B* 3.3

A woman of fortune, being used to the handling of money, spends it judiciously; but a woman who gets the command of money for the first time upon her marriage, has such a gust in spending it, that she throws it away with great profusion. *B* 3.3

A pretty woman may be foolish; a pretty woman may be wicked; a pretty woman may not like me. But there is no danger in marrying a pretty woman as is apprehended: she will not be persecuted if she does not invite persecution. A pretty woman, if she has a mind to be wicked, can find a readier way than another; and that is all. *B* 4.131

No money is better spent than what is laid out for domestic satisfaction. A man is pleased that his wife is drest as well as other people; and a wife is pleased that she is drest. *B* 2.352

My wife had a particular reverence for cleanliness, and desired the praise of neatness in her dress and furniture, as many ladies do, till they become troublesome to their best friends, slaves to their own besoms, and only sigh for the hour of sweeping their husbands out of the house as dirt and useless lumber. *JM* 1.247

Travel

A man who has not been in Italy, is always conscious of an inferiority, from his not having seen what it is expected a man should see. The grand object of travelling is to see the shores of the Mediterranean. *B* 3.36

Had this happened twenty years ago [the granting of his pension], I should have gone to Constantinople to learn Arabick, as Pococke did. *B* 4.27

An *Athenian* blockhead is the worst of all blockheads [of Oxford men who stay in Oxford]. *B* 1.73

There are two objects of curiosity, – the Christian world, and the Mahometan world. All the rest may be considered as barbarous. *B* 4.199

The use of travelling is to regulate imagination by reality, and instead of thinking how things may be, to see them as they are. *L* 1.254

Time may be employed to more advantage from nineteen to twenty-four almost in any way than in travelling. *B* 3.352

Worth seeing? Yes; but not worth going to see [the Giant's Causeway]. *B* 3.410

To go and see one druidical temple is only to see that it is nothing, for there is neither art nor power in it; and seeing one is as much as one could wish. *B* 5.132

Ay, that is the state of the world. Water is the same every where [to Boswell, who compared the Firth of Forth with Constantinople and the Bay of Naples]. *B* 5.54

Pray, Sir, have you ever seen Brentford? [to Adam Smith expatiating on the beauty of Glasgow]. *B* 4.186

He is gone, I believe, to a climate in which he will not find the country much warmer and the men much blacker than that he has left [of a Jamaica gentleman lately dead]. *JM* 2.302

Boswell: I do indeed come from Scotland, but I cannot help it ... Johnson: That, Sir, I find, is what a very great many of your countrymen cannot help. *B* 1.392

A tree might be a show in Scotland, as a horse in Venice. *WI*

Consider, sir, the value of such a *piece of timber* here [on losing his stick in Scotland]. *B* 5.319

I give you leave to say, and you may quote me for it, that there are more gentlemen in Scotland than there are shoes. *JM* 2.77

[Mr Ogilvie] observed, that Scotland had a great many noble wild prospects. Johnson: I believe, Sir, you have a great many. Norway, too, has noble wild prospects; and Lapland is remarkable for prodigious noble wild prospects. But, Sir, let me tell you, the noblest prospect which a Scotchman ever sees, is the high road that leads him to England! *B* 1.425

Their learning is like bread in a besieged town: every man gets a little, but no man gets a full meal. *B* 2.363

Describe it, Sir? [an inn] – Why, it was so bad that Boswell wished to be in Scotland. *B* 3.51

Come, let me know what it is that makes a Scotchman happy! [calling for a gill of whisky]. *B* 5.346

I will do you, Boswell, the justice to say, that you are the most *unscottified* of your countrymen. You are almost the only instance of a Scotchman that I have ever known who did not at every other sentence bring in some other Scotchman. *B* 2.242

The Irish are a *fair people*; – they never speak well of one another. *B* 2.307

Dublin, though a place much worse than London, is not so bad as Iceland. *B* 4.358

In Ireland no man visits where he cannot drink. *LP* 3.188

I am willing to love all mankind, *except an American*. *B* 3.290

Sir, two men of any other nation who are shown into a room together, at a house where they are both visitors, will immediately find some conversation. But two Englishmen will probably go each to a different window and remain in obstinate silence. Sir, we as yet do not enough understand the common rights of humanity. *B* 4.191

France is worse than Scotland in everything but climate. *B* 2.403

Now there, Sir, is the difference between an Englishman and a Frenchman. A Frenchman must be always talking, whether he knows any thing of the matter or not; an Englishman is content to say nothing, when he has nothing to say. *B* 4.14

Sir, I question if in Paris such a company as is sitting round this table could be got together in less than half a year. *B* 3.253

Sir, thus it is. This is the proportion. Let me see; forty times forty is sixteen hundred. As three to sixteen hundred, so is the proportion of an Englishman to a Frenchman [on being told that the French Academy had taken forty years to complete a task similar to the Dictionary: (in fact Johnson took seven or eight years)]. *B* 1.186

The French are a gross, ill-bred, untaught people; a lady there will spit on the floor and rub it with her foot. *B* 3.352

I am always sorry when any language is lost, because languages are the pedigree of nations. *B* 5.310

Whoever has once experienced the full flow of London talk, when he retires to country friendships and rural sports, must either be contented to turn again and play with the rattle, or he will pine away like a great fish in a little pond, and die for want of his usual food. *JM* 1.324

They who are content to live in the country are *fit* for the country. *B* 4.338

Why, Sir, you find no man, at all intellectual, who is willing to leave London. No, Sir, when a man is tired of London, he is tired of life; for there is in London all that life can afford. *B* 3.178

A country gentleman should bring his lady to visit London as soon as he can, that they may have agreeable topicks for conversation when they are by themselves. *B* 3.178

A small country town is not the place in which one would choose to quarrel with a wife; every human being in such a place is a spy. *L* 1.107

More can be had here [in London] for the money, even by ladies, than any where else. You cannot play tricks with your fortune in a small place; you must make an uniform appearance. Here a lady may have well-furnished apartments, and elegant dress, without any meat in her kitchen. *B* 3.378

Why, Sir, Fleet-street has a very animated appearance; but I think the full tide of human existence is at Charing-cross. *B* 2.337

Here falling houses thunder on your head,/And here a female atheist talks you dead. *Poems* ('London')

Music, Art & Pleasure

All animated Nature loves music – except myself! *B* 2.409n

The only sensual pleasure without vice [music]. *JM* 2.301

[Music] excites in my mind no ideas, and hinders me from contemplating my own. *JM* 2.103

If [music] softens the mind, so as to prepare it for the reception of salutary feelings, it may be good: but inasmuch as it is melancholy *per se,* it is bad. B 4.22

No man of talent, or whose mind was capable of better things, ever would devote his time and attention to so idle and frivolous a pursuit [music]. *JM* 2.404

Difficult do you call it, Sir? I wish it were impossible [on hearing a violin solo]. *JM* 2.308

There is nothing, I think, in which the power of art is shown so much as in playing the fiddle. *B* 2.226

Painting, Sir, can illustrate, but cannot inform. *B* 4.321

I had rather see the portrait of a dog that I know, than all the allegorical paintings they can show me in the world. *JM* 2.15

Sir, among the anfractuosities of the human mind I know not if it may not be one, that there is a superstitious reluctance to sit for a picture. *B* 4.4

Painting consumes labour not disproportionate to its effect; but a fellow will hack half a year at a block of marble to make something in stone that hardly resembles a man. The value of statuary is owing to its difficulty. You would not value the finest head cut upon a carrot. *B* 2.439

The labour of the savages of North America, but the amusement of the gentlemen of England [hunting]. *JM* 2.170

I am sorry I have not learnt to play at cards. It is very useful in life: it generates kindness and consolidates society. *B* 5.404

Sir, I am a great friend to public amusements; for they keep people from vice. You now [to Boswell] would have been with a wench, had you not been here [at the Pantheon]. *B* 2.169

Those who resist gaiety will be likely for the most part to fall a sacrifice to appetite. *JM* 1.219

Whoever thinks of going to bed before twelve o'clock is a scoundrel. *JM* 2.19

Some people have a foolish way of not minding, or pretending not to mind, what they eat. For my part, I mind my belly very studiously, and very carefully; for I look upon it, that he who does not mind his belly will hardly mind anything else. *B* 1.467

A man seldom thinks with more earnestness of anything than he does of his dinner; and if he cannot get that well dressed he should be suspected of inaccuracy in other things. *JM* 1.249

Sir, when a man is invited to dinner, he is disappointed if he does not get something good. *B* 3.186

This was a good enough dinner, to be sure; but it was not a dinner to *ask* a man to. *B* 1.470

Sir, we could not have had a better dinner had there been a *Synod of Cooks*. *B* 1.470

It will never do, Sir. There is nothing served about there, neither tea, nor coffee, nor lemonade, nor anything whatever; and depend upon it, Sir, a man does not love to go to a place from whence he comes out exactly as he went in. *B* 4.90

It is as bad as bad can be: it is ill-fed, ill-killed, ill-kept, and ill-drest [to a waiter, about mutton served at an inn]. *B* 4.284

Any of us would kill a cow, rather than not have beef. *B* 5.247

I wish I was a Jew ... because, I should then have the gust of eating it [pork], with the pleasure of sinning. *B* 4.292

It has been a common saying of physicians in England, that a cucumber should be well sliced, and dressed with pepper and vinegar, and then thrown out, as good for nothing. *B* 5.289

Drinking may be practised with great prudence; a man who exposes himself when he is intoxicated has not the art of getting drunk ... he is without skill in inebriation. *B* 3.389

I have heard him assert that a tavern chair was the throne of human felicity. *B* 2.152n

A man would be drowned by it before it made him drunk ... No, Sir, claret is the liquor for boys; port, for men; but he who aspires to be a hero (smiling) must drink brandy ... brandy will do soonest for a man what drinking *can* do for him. *B* 3.381

[On the truth of the saying *In vino veritas*] Why, Sir, that may be an argument for drinking if you suppose men in general to be liars. But, Sir, I would not keep company with a fellow who lies as long as he is sober, and whom you must make drunk before you can get a word of truth out of him. *B* 2.187

Idleness & Happiness

We would all be idle if we could. *B* 3.13

I have, all my life long, been lying till noon; yet I tell all young men, and tell them with great sincerity, that nobody who does not rise early will ever do any good. *B* 5.210

The happiest part of a man's life is what he passes lying awake in bed in the morning. *B* 5.252

To do nothing is in every man's power; we can never want an opportunity of omitting duties. *Ram* no. 155

The great direction which Burton has left to men disordered like you [Boswell], is this, *Be not solitary; be not idle*: which I would thus modify; – If you are idle, be not solitary; if you are solitary, be not idle. *B* 3.415

Solitude is dangerous to reason, without being favourable to virtue. *JM* 1.219

The solitary mortal is certainly luxurious, probably superstitious, and possibly mad. *JM* 1.219

When any fit of anxiety, or gloominess, or perversion of mind lays hold upon you, make it a rule not to publish it by complaints, but exert your whole care to hide it; by endeavouring to hide it, you will drive it away. Be always busy. *B* 3.368

I never considered whether I should be a grave man, or a merry man, but just let inclination, for the time, have its course. *B* 1.470

Employment, Sir, and hardships prevent melancholy. I suppose in all our army in America there was not one man who went mad. *B* 3.176

Keep yourself cheerful. Lie in bed with a lamp, and when you cannot sleep and are beginning to think, light your candle and read. *B* 4.409n

Grief is a species of idleness. *L* 1.212

The love of ease is always gaining upon age. *LP* 3.188

Sir, you cannot give me an instance of any man who is permitted to lay out his own time, contriving not to have tedious hours. *B* 2.194

There is nothing, Sir, too little for so little a creature as man; it is by studying little things that we attain the great art of having as little misery and as much happiness as possible. *B* 1.433

Money and time are the heaviest burdens of life, and the unhappiest of mortals are those who have more of either than they know how to use. *Idl* no. 30

Hope is itself a species of happiness and perhaps, the chief happiness in which this world affords; but, like other pleasures immoderately enjoyed, the excesses of hope must be expiated by pain. *B* 1.368

To-morrow is an old deceiver, and his cheat never grows stale. *L* 1.221

No sooner are we supplied with everything that nature can demand, than we sit down to contrive artificial appetites. *Idl* no. 30

Depend upon it, that if a man *talks* of his misfortunes, there is something in them that is not disagreeable to him; for where there is nothing but pure misery, there never is any recourse to the mention of it. *B* 4.31

The cure for the greatest part of human miseries is not radical, but palliative. *Ram* no. 32

It has been well observed, that the misery of man proceeds not from any single crush of overwhelming evil, but from small vexations continually repeated. *LP* 3.125

Wealth & Poverty

Sir, all the arguments which are brought to represent poverty as no evil show it to be evidently a great evil. You never find people labouring to convince you that you may live very happily upon a plentiful fortune. *B* 1.439

Poverty is very gently paraphrased by want of riches. In that sense, almost every man may, in his own opinion, be poor. But there is another poverty, which is want of competence of all that can soften the miseries of life, of all that can diversify attention or delight imagination. There is yet another poverty, which is want of necessaries, a species of poverty which no care of the public, no charity of particulars, can preserve many from feeling openly, and many secretly ... The milder degrees of poverty are, sometimes, supported by hope; but the more severe often sink down in motionless despondence. Life must be seen before it can be known. *W* 4.449

Life is a pill which none of us can bear to swallow without gilding; yet for the poor we delight in stripping it still barer, and are not ashamed to show even visible displeasure if ever the bitter taste is taken from their mouths. *JM* 1.205

It is an unhappy circumstance that one might give away five hundred pounds in a year to those that importune in the streets, and not do any good. *B* 4.3

Madam, to enable them to beg on [when asked by a lady why he so constantly gave money to beggars]. *JM* 2.393

It will be found upon a nearer view that they who extol the happiness of poverty do not mean the same state with those who deplore its miseries. *Ram* no. 202

He that sees before him to his third dinner, has a long prospect. *L* 1.392

Poverty takes away so many means of doing good, and produces so much inability to resist evil, both natural and moral, that it is by all virtuous means to be avoided. *B* 4.152

This mournful truth is ev'rywhere confess'd,/ Slow rises worth by poverty depress'd. *Poems* 76

Resolve not to be poor: whatever you have, spend less. Poverty is a great enemy to human happiness; it certainly destroys liberty, and it makes some virtues impracticable and others extremely difficult. *B* 4.157

A man who both spends and saves money is the happiest man, because he has both enjoyments. *B* 3.322

There is no being so poor and so contemptible, who does not think there is somebody still poorer, and still more contemptible. *B* 2.13

Sir, the insolence of wealth will creep out. *B* 3.316

A decent provision for the poor, is the true test of civilisation. *B* 2.130

It is better to *live* rich than to *die* rich. *B* 3.304

There are few ways in which a man can be more innocently employed than in getting money. *B* 2.323

Getting money is not all a man's business: to cultivate kindness is a valuable part of the business of life. *B* 3.182

There is no condition which is not disquieted either with the care of gaining or of keeping money; and the race of man may be divided in a political estimate between those who are practising fraud and those who are repelling it. *Ram* no. 131

The only great instance that I have ever known of the enjoyment of wealth was that of Jamaica Dawkins, who, going to visit Palmyra, and hearing that the way was infested by robbers, hired a troop of Turkish horses to guard him. *B* 4.126

Many there are who openly and almost professedly regulate all their conduct by their love of money; who have no other reason for action or forbearance, for compliance or refusal, than that they hope to gain more by one than by the other. These are indeed the meanest and cruellest of human beings, a race with whom, as with some pestiferous animals, the whole creation seems to be at war; but who, however detested or scorned, long continue to add heap to heap, and when they have reduced one to beggary, are still permitted to fasten on another. *Ram* no. 175

Praise [and] money, the two corrupters of mankind. *B* 4.242

Boswell, *lend* me sixpence – *not to be repaid*. *B* 4.191

We are not here to sell a parcel of boilers and vats, but the potentiality of growing rich beyond the dreams of avarice [on being asked the value of Thrale's brewery]. *B* 4.87

Politics

Sir, that is all visionary. I would not give half a guinea to live under one form of government rather than another. It is of no moment to the happiness of an individual. *B* 2.170

Publick affairs vex no man. *B* 4.220

Why, Sir, most schemes of political improvement are very laughable things. *B* 2.102

All intellectual improvement arises from leisure: all leisure arises from one working for another. *B* 2.219

Depend upon it, Sir, every state of society is as luxurious as it can be. Men always take the best they can get. *B* 3.282

Sir, you are a young man, but I have seen a great deal of the world, and take it upon my word and experience, that where you see a Whig you see a rascal. *JM* 2.393

I saved appearances tolerably well; but I took care that the *Whig dogs* should not have the best of it [when praised for his impartiality in writing up the parliamentary debates]. *B* 1.504

The first Whig was the Devil. *B* 3.326

Whiggism is a negation of all principle. *B* 1.431

He's a Whig, Sir, a sad dog. *B* 3.271

Whiggism [is] latterly no better than the politics of stock-jobbers, and the religion of infidels. *B* 2.117

Sir, Hume is a Tory by chance – as being a Scotchman; but not upon a principle of duty; for he has no principle. If he is any thing he is a Hobbist. *B* 5.272

Johnson: Mason's a Whig. Mrs Knowles, (not hearing distinctly:) What! a prig, Sir? Johnson: Worse, Madam; a Whig! But he is both. *B* 3.294

Pulteney was a paltry fellow. He was a Whig who pretended to be honest; and you know it is ridiculous for a Whig to pretend to be honest. He cannot hold it out. *B* 5.339

Sir, he is a cursed Whig, a *bottomless* Whig, as they all are now [Burke]. *B* 4.223

Patriotism is the last refuge of a scoundrel. *B* 2.348

[No man is] more an enemy to public peace, than he who fills weak heads with imaginary claims, and breaks the series of civil subordination, by inciting the lower classes of mankind to encroach upon the higher. *B* 2.244

Sir, your levellers wish to level *down* as far as themselves; but they cannot bear levelling *up* to themselves. They would all have some people under them; why not then have some people above them? *B* 1.448

Sir, I would no more deprive a nobleman of his respect, than of his money. I consider myself as acting a part in the great system of society, and I do to others as I would have them do to me. I would behave to a nobleman as I should expect he would behave to me, were I a nobleman and he Sam Johnson. *B* 1.447

Few lords will cheat; and, if they do, they'll be ashamed of it: farmers cheat and are not ashamed of it: they have all the sensual vices of the nobility, with cheating into the bargain. There is as much fornication and adultery amongst farmers as amongst noblemen. *B* 3.353

It is better that some should be happy, than that none should be happy, which would be the case in a general state of equality. *B* 3.26

So far is it from being true that men are naturally equal, that no two people can be half an hour together, but one shall acquire an evident superiority over the other. *B* 2.13

We are all agreed as to our own liberty; we would have as much of it as we can get; but we are not agreed as to the liberty of others; for in proportion as we take, others must lose. *B* 3.383

It has been observed that they who most loudly clamour for liberty do not most liberally grant it. *LP* 1.135

How is it that we hear the loudest *yelps* for liberty among the drivers of negroes? *B* 3.201

The notion of liberty amuses the people of England, and helps to keep off the *taedium vitae*. When a butcher tells you that *his heart bleeds for his country*, he has, in fact, no uneasy feeling. *B* 1.394

A country governed by a despot is an inverted cone. *B* 3.283

All distant power is bad. *B* 4.213

The true state of every nation is the state of common life. *B* 5.109

The age is running mad after innovation; all the business of the world is to be done in a new way; men are to be hanged in a new way; Tyburn itself is not safe from the fury of innovation [on the abolition of public executions]. *B* 4.188

George the First knew nothing, and desired to know nothing; did nothing, and desired to do nothing: and the only good thing that is told of him is, that he wished to restore the crown to its hereditary successor. *B* 2.342

The finest gentleman I have ever seen [George III]. *B* 2.40

Is any king a Whig? *L* 2.87

Sir, I think that the pleasure of cursing the House of Hanover, and drinking King James's health, are amply overbalanced by three hundred pounds a year [of his pension]. *B* 1.429

Philosophy & Religion

I challenge it *thus* [on kicking a stone to refute Berkeley's theory of the non-existence of matter]. *B* 1.471

Pray, Sir, don't leave us; for we may perhaps forget to think of you, and then you will cease to exist [to a Berkleyan]. *B* 4.27

Sir, we *know* our will is free, and *there's* an end on't. *B* 2.82

To be prejudiced is always to be weak; yet there are prejudices so near to laudable that they have been often praised and are always pardoned. *W* 6.225

Rousseau, Sir, is a very bad man. I would sooner sign a sentence for his transportation, than that of any felon who has gone from the Old Bailey these many years. Yes, I should like to have him work in the plantations. Boswell: Sir, do you think him as bad a man as Voltaire? Johnson: Why, Sir, it is difficult to settle the proportion of inquity between them. *B* 2.12

And as to Hume, – a man who has so much conceit as to tell all mankind that they have been bubbled for ages, and he is the wise man who sees better than they, – a man who has so little scrupulosity as to venture to oppose those principles which have been thought necessary to human happiness, – is he to be surprised if another man comes and laughs at him? If he is the great man he thinks himself, all this cannot hurt him: it is like throwing peas against a rock. *B* 5.29

Johnson: As I cannot be *sure* that I have fulfilled the conditions on which salvation is granted, I am afraid I may be one of those who shall be damned (looking dismally). Dr. Adams: What do you mean by damned? Johnson (passionately and loudly): Sent to Hell, Sir, and punished everlastingly. *B* 4.299

I should not think the better of a man who should tell me on his death-bed he was sure of salvation. *B* 3.295

It is our first duty to serve society, and, after we have done that, we may attend wholly to the salvation of our own souls. A youthful passion for abstracted devotion should not be encouraged. *B* 2.10

I am no friend to making religion appear too hard. Many good people have done harm, by giving severe notions of it. *B* 5.316

Scruples [make] many men miserable, but few men good. *JM* 2.153

You must consider laxity is a bad thing; but preciseness is also a bad thing; and your general character may be more hurt by preciseness than by dining with a Bishop in Passion-week. *B* 4.89

All argument is against it; but all belief is for it [the existence of ghosts]. *B* 3.230

Boswell: Would you not, sir, start as Mr. Garrick does, if you saw a ghost? Johnson: I hope not. If I did, I should frighten the ghost. *B* 5.38

I do not know, Sir, that the fellow is an infidel; but if he be an infidel, he is an infidel as a dog is an infidel; that is to say, he has never thought upon the subject [Foote]. *B* 2.95

Campbell is a good man, a pious man. I am afraid he has not been in the inside of a church for many years, but he never passes a church without pulling off his hat. This shews that he has good principles [Dr John Campbell] *B* 1.417

He insisted on people praying with him; and I'd as lief pray with Kit Smart as any one else. Another charge was, that he did not love clean linen; and I have no passion for it. *B* 1.397

I would be a Papist if I could. I have fear enough; but an obstinate rationality prevents me. *B* 4.289

I wonder that women are not all Papists. *B* 4.289

For my part, Sir, I think all Christians, whether Papists or Protestants, agree in the essential articles, and that their differences are trivial, and rather political than religious. *B* 1.405

A man who is converted from Protestantism to Popery, may be sincere: he parts with nothing: he is only superadding to what he already had. But a convert from Popery to Protestantism, gives up so much of what he has held as sacred as any thing that he retains; there is so much *laceration of mind.* *B* 2.105

Every man who attacks my belief, diminishes in some degree my confidence in it, and therefore makes me uneasy; and I am angry with him who makes me uneasy. *B* 3.10

Truth, Sir, is a cow, which will yield such people [sceptics] no more milk, and so they are gone to milk the bull. *B* 1.444

A man who is good enough to go to heaven is good enough to be a clergyman. *B* 2.171

A bishop has nothing to do at a tippling house. *B* 4.75

I do not much like to see a Whig in any dress; but I hate to see a Whig in a parson's gown. *B* 5.255

I have always considered a clergyman as the father of a larger family than he is able to maintain. I would rather have Chancery suits upon my hands than the care of souls. *B* 2.342

This merriment of parsons is mighty offensive [of a company of clergymen who assumed 'the lax jollity of men of the world']. *B* 4.76

Be not too hasty to trust or to admire the teachers of morality: they discourse like angels but they live like men. *Ras* ch. 18

Sir, are you so grossly ignorant of human nature, as not to know that a man may be very sincere in good principles, without having good practice? *B* 5.359

Why, Sir, a man grows better humoured as he grows older. He improves by experience. When young, he thinks himself of great consequence and everything of importance. As he advances in life, he learns to think himself of no consequence and little things of little importance; and so he becomes more patient, and better pleased. *B* 5.211

The miseries of life would be increased beyond all human power of endurance if we were to enter the world with the same opinions as we carry from it. *Ram* no. 196

As I know more of mankind I expect less of them, and am ready now to call a man *a good man,* upon easier terms than I was formerly. *B* 4.239

There is a wicked inclination in most people to suppose an old man decayed in his intellects. If a young or middle-aged man, when leaving a company, does not recollect where he laid his hat, it is nothing; but if the same inattention is discovered in an old man, people will shrug their shoulders and say, 'His memory is going.' *B* 4.181

They are always telling lies of us old fellows. *B* 3.303

There is nothing against which an old man should be so much upon his guard as putting himself to nurse. *B* 2.474

Death

To my question, whether we might not fortify our minds for the approach of death, he answered, in a passion, 'No Sir, let it alone. It matters not how a man dies, but how he lives. The act of dying is not of importance, it lasts so short a time … A man knows it must be so, and submits. It will do him no good to whine.' *B* 2.106

No rational man can die without uneasy apprehension. *B* 3.294

I know not whether I should wish to have a friend by me, or have it all between God and myself. *B* 2.93

Boswell: But is not the fear of death natural to man?
Johnson: So much so, Sir, that the whole of life is but keeping away the thoughts of it. *B* 2.93

To neglect at any time preparation for death is to sleep on our post at a siege; but to omit it in old age is to sleep at an attack. *Ram* no. 78

If one was to think constantly of death the business of life would stand still. *B* 5.316

The death of great men is not always proportioned to the lustre of their lives ... The death of Pope was imputed by some of his friends to a silver saucepan, in which it was his delight to heat potted lampreys. *LP* 3.99

I said, I had reason to think that the thought of annihilation gave Hume no pain. Johnson: It was not so, Sir. He had a vanity in being thought easy. It is more probable that he should assume an appearance of ease, than that so very improbable a thing should be, as a man not afraid of going (as, in spite of his delusive theory, he cannot be sure but he may go,) into an unknown state, and not being uneasy at leaving all he knew. And you are to consider, that upon his own principle of annihilation he had no motive to speak the truth. *B* 3.153

I am disappointed by that stroke of death, which has eclipsed the gaiety of nations, and impoverished the publick stock of harmless pleasure [the death of Garrick]. *B* 4.360

When Death's pale horse runs away with persons on full speed, an active physician may possibly give them a turn; but if he carries them on an even slow pace, down hill too! no care nor skill can save them! *JM* 1.276

I struggle hard for life. I take physick, and take air; my friend's chariot is always ready. We have run this morning twenty-four miles, and could run forty-eight more. *But who can run the race with death?* [letter of 4 September 1784]. *B* 4.360